My Underground Home

Leanne Murner

Illustrated by Natalie Herington

PLANETARY EDUCATION
Fennell Bay, NSW, 2283 Australia

First published by Planetary Education 2022
Copyright © Leanne Murner

Cover design and Illustrations© Natalie Herington 2022
Natalie Herington -Bird Valley Illustration & Design
Printed in Australia

ISBN 978-0-6456435-1-0

A catalogue record is available from the
National Library of Australia

www.planetaryeducation.com.au

Dedication

I would like to dedicate this book to my 5 boys.

Oliver, Luca, Franki, Loui and Leo.

Thank you for being my inspiration and
being on this journey with me.

I am an earthworm; I live underground. You will always find me in a place where there is plenty of food, oxygen and moisture.

I don't have a nose, but I don't breathe through my mouth.
I breathe through my skin.
I have a coating of mucus over my skin that helps me to breathe.

I have a strong muscular mouth with no teeth.
I don't even have eyes!
I move through the soil using my muscles and small
bristles on my skin.

We speed up the breakdown of dead roots, leaves, grasses,
manure and food waste to feed the earth,
we are known for being earthworm engineers
and help with water movement through the soil.

We can eat up to one third our body weight in a day and we are also a great source of food for numerous animals, like birds, rats, and toads.

Have you ever seen some of us with a big swollen band around our body?
You might think this is where we have been chopped in half by a shovel, but this is a cocoon full of worm embryos.

I will shed my top layer of mucus and leave the cocoon in the soil. Depending on the environment, the eggs will hatch within 2 to 11 weeks.

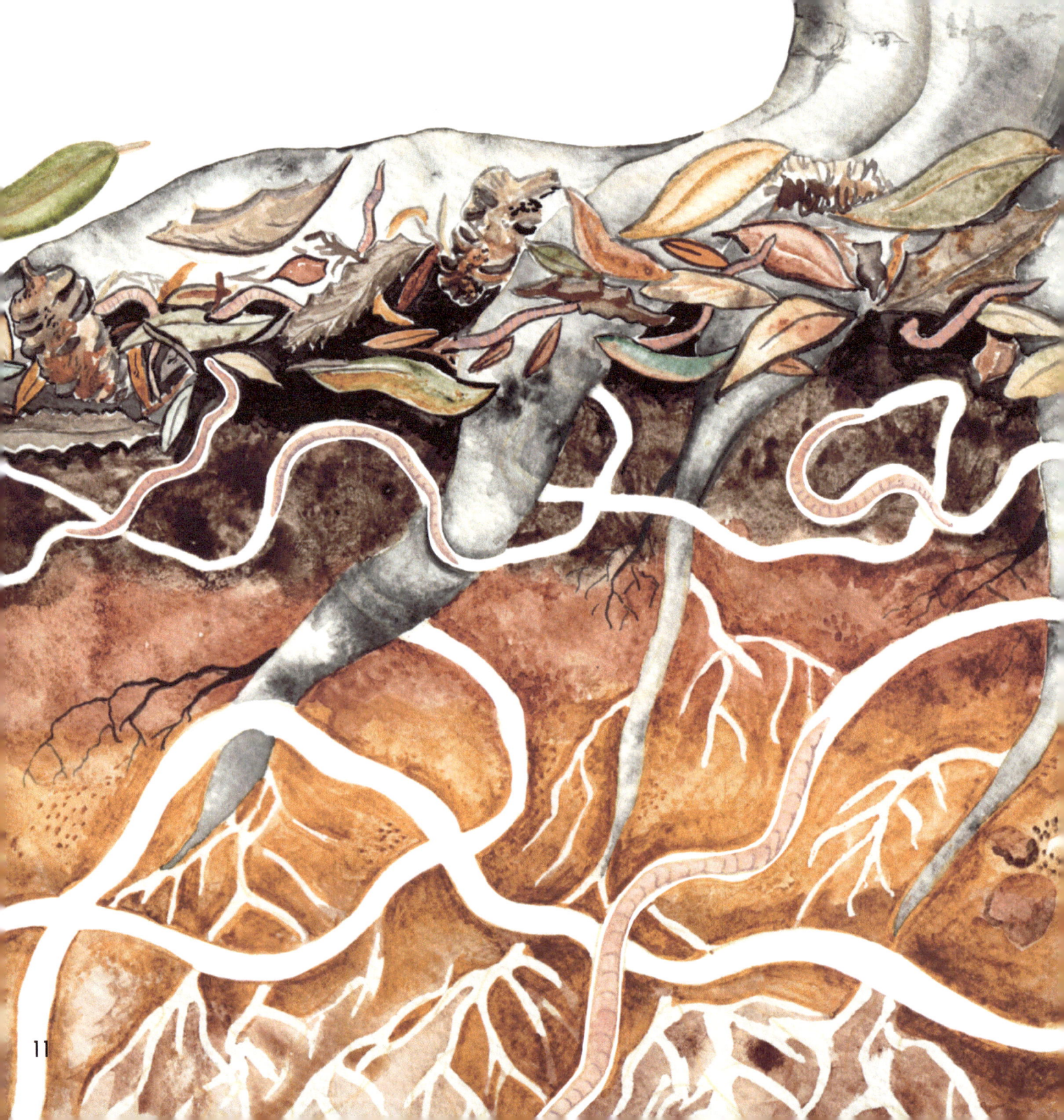

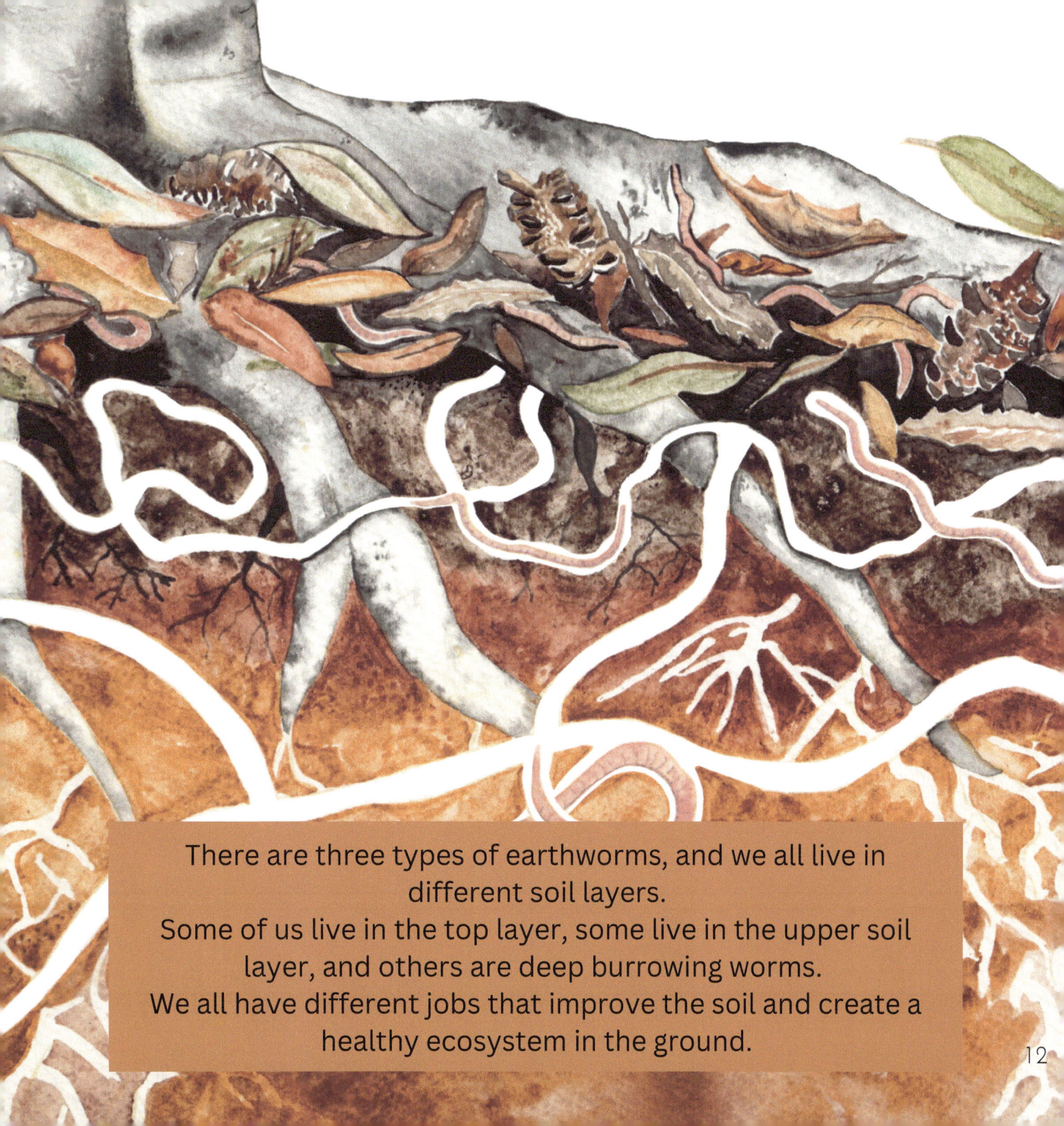

There are three types of earthworms, and we all live in different soil layers.
Some of us live in the top layer, some live in the upper soil layer, and others are deep burrowing worms.
We all have different jobs that improve the soil and create a healthy ecosystem in the ground.

I am a top-layer worm living in the subsoil. You will also find me on the top of the soil feeding on plant debris on the forest floor, living in leaf piles, eating other decaying plant matter, or in your compost and worm farm.

I love to break down food waste. I munch away at all the organic matter, turning it into compost. I like to stay on the surface, especially in the worm farm and compost. I make burrows through all the food scraps, helping break them down.

The second type is the upper-soil worms. These worms live around plant roots. Areas like this are rich with decaying roots and fungi. You will not see these worms as they don't venture above the ground.

Upper-soil worms can have burrows up to 60cm deep, making channels that help water travel deeper into the soil. These channels are filled with their waste, and this helps feed the roots of the plants.

The final type is the earthworm worker, also known as the night crawler. These worms travel at night and have permanent burrows that can be up to seven meters long. These are the ones you will likely see in your garden. They are busy tilling the soil, making it airier and nicer for the plants to grow.

These worms mainly feed on soil and leaf litter that they pull down into their burrows. They leave a plug made from a leaf, organic matter, or their waste at the entrance of their tunnel.

Have you ever seen a mound of dirt on the ground that looks like it's been pushed out from the inside? This little pile is an entrance to a worm's burrow, so be sure to leave it alone as it's a home.

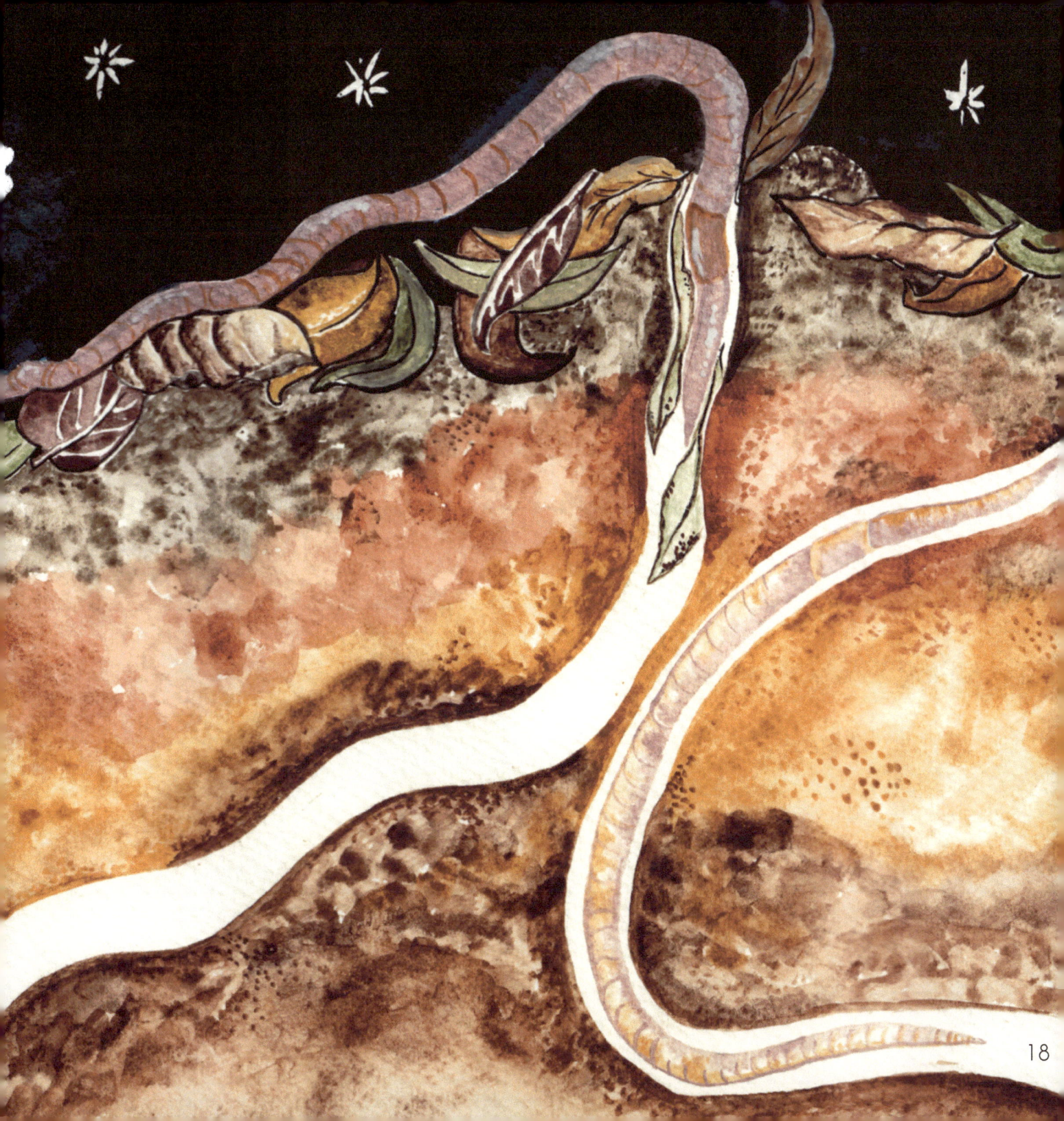

Covering the ground with mulch, leaves or grass clippings helps protect us from the heat and keeps the soil moist.

It is easy for us to work when our environment is cool and damp, so a lid on your worm farm is a great idea too.

Did you know it's not just worms that live in the soil? We share our home with a range of other insects and creatures.
There are spiders that live in the ground as well as slugs and beetles.

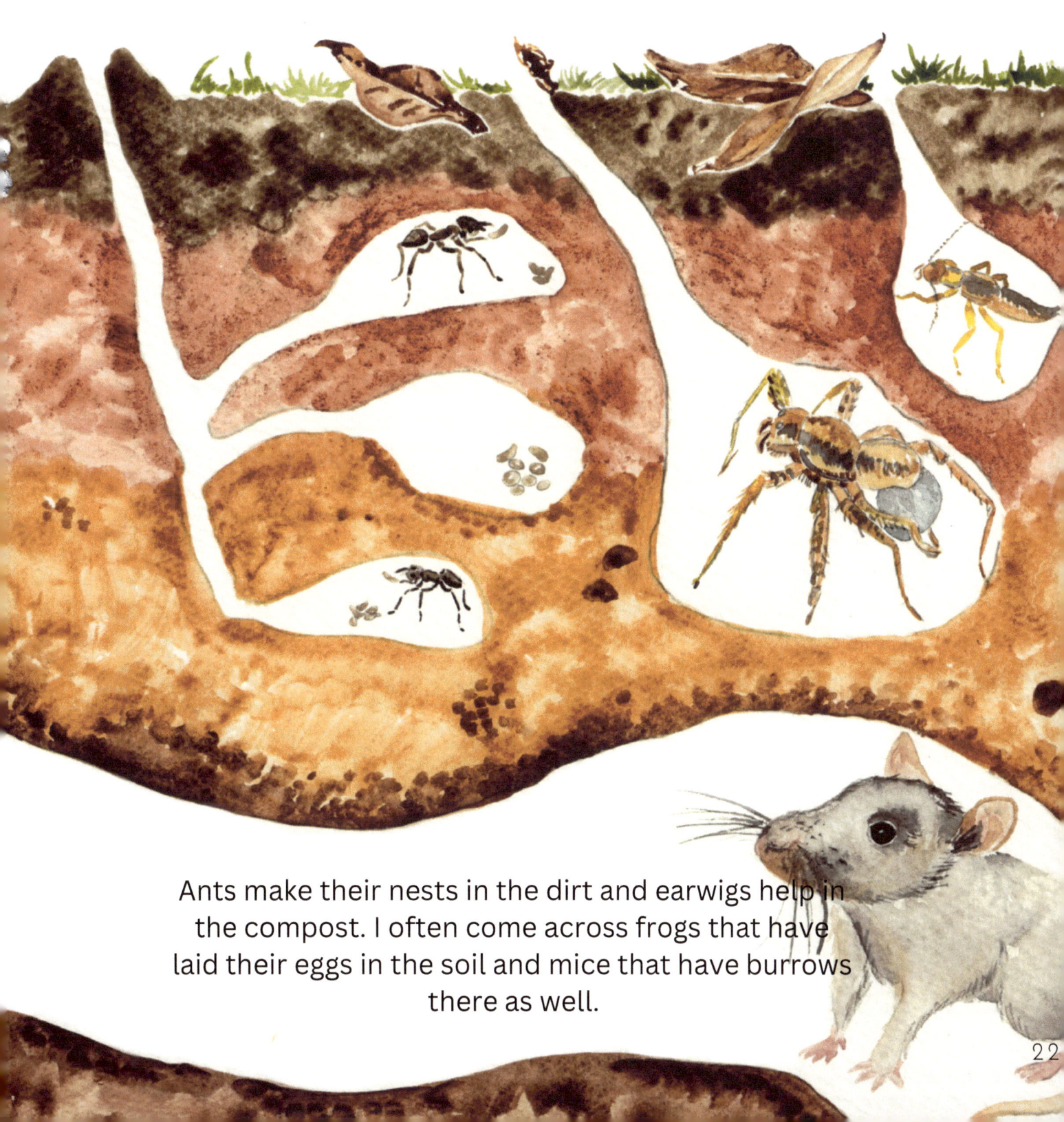

Ants make their nests in the dirt and earwigs help in the compost. I often come across frogs that have laid their eggs in the soil and mice that have burrows there as well.

Soil is home to thousands of animals, many are too small to be seen, but every single one is important to a healthy ecosystem.

We speed up the breakdown of dead roots, leaves, grasses, manure, and food waste. If our environment is healthy, we can easily turn waste into nutrients that feed the soil and help all plants to grow.

Oxygen – is a tasteless gas that is essential for our survival. When we breathe in oxygen, we exhale carbon dioxide. Plants and trees take in carbon dioxide as a source of carbon which they use to help them grow and they return the oxygen back into the atmosphere.

Moisture – is a form of water vapour.

Mucus – is a lubricant made mostly from water. This stops the skin of the worm from drying out.

Cocoon – is the outer layer of the egg casing. A cocoon can hold multiple eggs and will protect the eggs until they are hatched.

Embryo – is an unborn or unhatched offspring still in the process of development.

Plant debris – offcuts of grass, leaves, shrubbery, vines or tree branches. This can also be what has fallen off living plants and landed on the ground.

Organic matter – is anything that was alive and is now in, or on, the soil and starting to break down.

Fungi – a group of living organisms. They live all over the earth - on land, in the water, in air and on plants and animals.

Channels – Earthworms eat their way through the soil creating channels, or passageways, in the ground.

Tilling – loosening the soil. This action lets water flow through the soil more easily.

Ecosystem – insects, animals and plants working with non-living lings like soil, water and air to create a healthy life for all.

www.ingramcontent.com/pod-product-compliance
Lightning Source LLC
Chambersburg PA
CBHW041547260326

41914CB00016B/1576